CELEBRATING THE
NAME JUDE

Celebrating the Name Jude

Walter the Educator

Silent King Books

SILENT KING BOOKS

SKB

dedicated to everyone with the first
name of Jude

JUDE

The stars align in cosmic rhyme,

JUDE

To celebrate this name sublime.

JUDE

For Jude, a light that never fades,

JUDE

A beacon through the shifting shades.

JUDE

The poets sing, the minstrels play,

JUDE

In honor of Jude's wondrous way.

JUDE

A name that holds the world's embrace,

JUDE

A symbol of enduring grace.

JUDE

In every heart, in every soul,

JUDE

Jude's name, a piece that makes us whole.

JUDE

It bridges gaps, it mends the seams,

JUDE

It fuels our hopes, it shapes our dreams.

JUDE

From ancient stones to future's reach,

JUDE

Jude's name inspires, it does beseech.

JUDE

A call to live with truth and might,

JUDE

To walk the path, to seek the light.

JUDE

The winds that whisper through the pines,

JUDE

They speak of Jude in soft designs.

JUDE

A tale of wonder, love, and pride,

JUDE

An endless song that does abide.

JUDE

In Jude, we find a legacy,

JUDE

A name that shines eternally.

JUDE

With every breath, with every beat,

JUDE

It carves a path, both strong and sweet.

JUDE

So here we stand, with hearts aglow,

JUDE

To celebrate the name we know.

JUDE

Jude, a gem in life's vast sea,

JUDE

A timeless tale of harmony.

JUDE

In echoes of the past's embrace,

JUDE

In future's bright and boundless space,

JUDE

Jude's name will shine, a guiding star,

JUDE

A beacon near, a light afar.

JUDE

A name that holds the world's delight,

JUDE

A tapestry in colors bright.

JUDE

For Jude, a symbol pure and true,

JUDE

A cherished name in all we do.

JUDE

From dawn to dusk, from night to day,

JUDE

In every step along the way,

JUDE

The name of Jude will always be,

JUDE

A song of hope, a symphony.

JUDE

ABOUT THE CREATOR

Walter the Educator is one of the pseudonyms for Walter Anderson. Formally educated in Chemistry, Business, and Education, he is an educator, an author, a diverse entrepreneur, and he is the son of a disabled war veteran. "Walter the Educator" shares his time between educating and creating. He holds interests and owns several creative projects that entertain, enlighten, enhance, and educate, hoping to inspire and motivate you.

Follow, find new works, and stay up to date
with Walter the Educator™
at WaltertheEducator.com

www.ingramcontent.com/pod-product-compliance
Lightning Source LLC
LaVergne TN
LVHW010622070526
838199LV00063BA/5238